SYSTEMOLOGY
BIOFEEDBACK

POCKET EDITION

Published from
Mardukite Borsippa HQ, San Luis Valley, Colorado
Mardukite Academy & Systemology Society
for spiritual or philosophical purposes only

SYSTEMOLOGY BIOFEEDBACK

SPIRITUAL TECHNOLOGY FOR ASCENSION

Advanced Training Supplement
developed by Joshua Free for
the Systemology Society

THE JOSHUA FREE IMPRINT
JFI PUBLICATIONS

© 2024, JOSHUA FREE

ISBN : 978-1-961509-45-0

This manual is restricted to students using:
The Systemology Professional Course -or-
The Advanced Training Course

Portions of this book were excerpted from:
"The Way of the Wizard" by Joshua Free

First Edition Pocket Paperback — *February 2024*

mardukite.com

Take Systemology to the Next Level!

The Official Mardukite Systemology "Biofeedback Manual" is now available to the public for the very first time.

Seekers working on the "Pathway to Ascension" using the Systemology "Professional Course" and "Advanced Training Course" can discover how monitoring "biofeedback" responses while applying Systemology techniques can provide an even more advanced level of spiritual defragmentation.

Learn how electronic devices that measure "galvanic skin response" (GSR) or "electro-dermal response" (EDR) can enhance the effectiveness of our methods of spiritual processing whether "flying-solo" or working with a co-pilot.

This expanded edition of the original manual includes advice for advanced Systemologists on using GSR-Meters to assist defragmenting hidden areas of "energetic turbulence" such as the "spiritual implants" introduced in the Professional Course and A.T. materials.

Fundamentals of Systemology
Basic Course Lesson Booklet Series

#1 – *Being More Than Human*
#2 – *Realities In Agreement*
#3 – *Windows To Experience*
#4 – *Ancient Systemology*
#5 – *A History of Systemology*
#6 – *Systemology Processing*

The Pathway to Ascension
Professional Course Lesson Booklet Series

#1 – *Increasing Awareness*
#2 – *Thought & Emotion*
#3 – *Clear Communication*
#4 – *Handling Humanity*
#5 – *Free Your Spirit*
#6 – *Escaping Spirit-Traps*
#7 – *Eliminating Barriers*
#8 – *Conquest of Illusion*
#9 – *Confronting the Past*
#10 – *Lifting the Veils*
#11 – *Spiritual Implants*
#12 – *Games and Universes*
#13 – *Spiritual Energy*
#14 – *Spiritual Machinery*
#15 – *The Arcs of Infinity*
#16 – *Alpha Thought*

TABLET OF CONTENTS

INTRODUCTION TO THE MANUAL

– Introducing the Manual . . . 11
– The Three States of Knowingness . . . 13
– Charting Flights on the Pathway . . . 17
– Taking Flight on the Pathway . . . 19

SYSTEMOLOGY BIOFEEDBACK:
THE MANUAL

– Systemology and GSR-Biofeedback . . . 25
– The History and Development
    of GSR-Biofeedback Metering . . . 31
– Understanding GSR-Biofeedback
    for Spiritual Defragmentation . . . 43
– Understanding GSR-Meters
    and Knowing How To Read Them . . . 53
– Reading GSR-Biofeedback Meters . . . 60
– Applying GSR-Meters
    to Systematic Processing . . . 67

APPENDIX

– Glossary . . . 81
– Additional Resources . . . 99

INTRODUCTION TO
THE MANUAL

This manual is restricted to students using:
The Systemology Professional Course -or-
The Advanced Training Course

INTRODUCING THE SYSTEMOLOGY BIOFEEDBACK MANUAL

Mardukite Systemology is a new evolution in Human understanding about the "systems" governing *Life, Reality,* the *Universe* and all *Existences*. It is also a *Spiritual Path* used to transcend the Human experience and reach *"Ascension."*

This is an advanced professional course supplement (manual) detailing how to *apply* physical technology to our spiritual philosophy to enhance a *Seeker's* personal progress on the *"Pathway" to Ascension.*

This manual supplements our *Professional Course* series of lessons—available as individual booklets, or collected in two volumes titled *"The Pathway to Ascension"* The *Professional Course* follows after material given in the *Basic Course* booklets, or *"Fundamentals of Systemology"* volume.

The systematic methodology that we use to assist an individual to increase their *"Actualized Awareness"* (and reach gradually higher toward their *"Spiritual Ascension"*) is referred to as *"The Pathway"* — and that individual is called a *"Seeker."*

To receive the greatest benefit from this manual: it is expected that a *Seeker* will already be familiar with the fundamental concepts and terminology (previously relayed in the *Basic Course* and *Professional Course* lessons) of our *applied philosophy.*

As a *Seeker* increases their *Awareness* in this lifetime, their spiritual *"Knowingness"* also increases—which is to say their *certainty* on *Life,* on this and other *Universes,* and on *realizing Self* as an unlimited "spiritual being" *having* an enforced restrictive "human experience." A *Seeker* also *knowingly* increases their command and control of the "human experience." And this is a part of what is meant by *"Actualized Awareness."*

THREE STATES OF KNOWINGNESS

Raising a *Seeker's* level of *Actualized Awareness* requires, by definition, "bringing what is *hidden* (or not consciously known) up into the realm of *light* or *Knowingness*." We might go as far to say, as an imperfect example, that there are three primary states of *Knowingness*: *actual knowing*, *almost knowing* and *not-knowing*.

Actual knowing is what an individual is conscious of and can easily recall as needed. It makes up our "surface" (or "above-the-surface") thoughts; what is *"actually known"* and available to *Self* for "inspection" or analytical thought. This includes what we have *certainty* on as part of our *reality*.

Then, there are other *things* "below-the-surface" that we do not easily remember

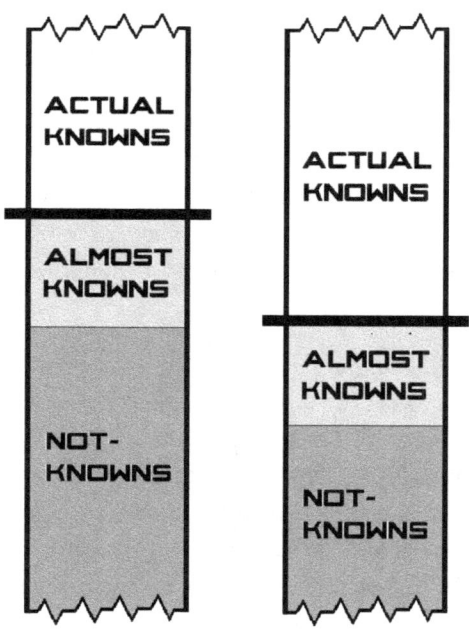

(or have any *reality* on)—and these fit our other categories of *almost knowing* and *not-knowing*. One key difference between these other two states is how *far* "below-the-surface" a *thing* is.

What you *"almost know"* are those *things* just "below-the-surface"—so *close* to the "surface" that they are almost accessible. This "gray area" includes what an individual is *uncertain* of. With a little assistance (*"Systematic Processing"* techniques), you can actually move a *thing* that is *"almost known"* to an "above-the-surface" state of *"actually knowing"* or remembering again. Only then may it be treated with any *certainty*.

There are also memories very deeply buried "below-the-surface." This includes suppressed data that is not currently accessible—and therefore, presently *"not-known."* Once again, there is a way to move *things* from this state into another state. For this to happen, the previous *"almost known" things* ("just-below-the-surface") need to be "purged" (at least partially) by *"resurfacing"* them into *"actually known" things*.

As more layers of *"almost knowns"* are *resurfaced* into *"actual knowns,"* more of what is *"not-known"* becomes accessible within the "gray area." *Systematic Processing* techniques of *Systemology* are intended to target this "gray area" — promoting increased *realizations* by elevating more *knowledge* and *present-time attention* to a state of *Actual Awareness*.

What is already *"known"* is easily accessed with *systematic processing*. When using <u>*Biofeedback*</u> technology, we are most interested in the *"almost knowns,"* This area is accessible with <u>*Biofeedback*</u> even when a *Seeker* is not yet fully *aware* of it. But, more deeply buried *"not-knowns"* are still not accessible until more layers come off and they become *"almost knowns."*

CHARTING FLIGHTS ON THE PATHWAY

Although there is a systematic structure to *fragmentation*, the personal journey experienced along the *Pathway* will be different for each *Seeker*. For example, certain areas will seem more *"turbulent"* or difficult for one *Seeker* than another. We tend to say that these areas have more *"charge"* on them—or that they are more *"heavily charged."* It is best to handle such areas when you are already feeling "good" and not in a situation (or condition) where that specific area is consistently being *"triggered"* or *"restimulated."*

As an applied philosophy, *Systemology* "theory" can be easily utilized in the "laboratory" of the "world-at-large" in everyday life. This is implied within the basic instruction of each lesson. Unlike other "sciences" that conduct experiments by making a change to some "objective variable" *out there* and waiting to see an effect, our focus is the individual (or *Observer*) themselves, and how *they* affect the "*Reality*" perceived.

Our philosophy is applied by using specific exercises and systematic techniques. These "*processes*" provide the most stable personal gain (and *realizations*) for each area; but only when actually applied with a *Seeker's* full "*presence*" and *Awareness*. Hundreds of such *processes* may be found in the "*Pathway to Ascension*" (*Professional Course*) material.

Applying a technique is called "*running a process*." *Processes* are designed with very simple instructions or "*command-lines*." To *run* a *processing command-line*, a *Seeker* may be assisted by the communication of that *line* from a "*Co-Pilot*" (as in "*Traditional Piloting*"). But even then, a *Seeker* must still personally "input" the *command* as *Self*. For this reason — and quite thankfully — *Solo-Processing* is possible.

TAKING FLIGHT ON THE PATHWAY

Processing Techniques are intended to treat the *Spiritual Being* or *Alpha-Spirit*; the individual themselves. The *"command-lines"* are *directed to* the individual themselves—not some *mental machinery* of theirs, and not even a <u>*Biofeedback*</u> metering device.

Systematic Processing is applied by the *Alpha-Spirit*—who then *Self-directs* command of their "Mind-System" or "body" (*genetic-vehicle*), both of which are "constructs" that the *Alpha-Spirit* (*Self*, or the "I-AM" *Awareness unit*) operates, but neither of which is actually *Self*. *Fragmentation* causes *Humans* to falsely identify *Self as* the "*Mind*" or even a "*Body.*"

Some *processes* can be treated quite lightly at first; others may require a bit of working at in order to get *"running"* well. It is important to set aside a period of time when you can be dedicated to your studies and *processing*. This period of time is referred to as a *"processing session."* When a *process* does start *running* well, it is important to be able to complete it to a satisfactory *"end-point."*

Processing allows us to be able to *actually* "look" at *things* and even determine the *considerations* we have made—or attitudes we have decided—about *Reality* as a result of those experiences.

It doesn't do us much good to simply "glance"—or to *restimulate* something uncomfortable and then quickly *withdraw* from it once again, leaving more of our *attention* yet again behind and held fixedly on it.

Generally speaking, a *Seeker* continues to *run* a *process* so long as something is "happening"—which is to say, the *process* is still producing a change. Usually this is evident by the type of "answers" that a *command-line* prompts a *Seeker* to originate from the database of their own *Mind-System*.

Processing Command-Lines ("PCL") are not "magic words"; they do not "do" anything on their own. They systematically assist a *Seeker* to direct their own attention toward increasing *Awareness*.

A *Seeker* may also cease to generate new "data" from a *process* without reaching an *"ultimate"* realization as an *"end-point."* It is possible that additional "layers" (or even other "areas") require handling before anything "deeper" is accessible. If this is the case, end the *process*. But, if a *Seeker* is *withdrawing* from something uncomfortable that was incited or stirred up, then a *process* is *run* until they feel "good" about it.

One of the benefits to *Flying-Solo* on the *Pathway* is that the *processing* is entirely *Self-determined*. This naturally provides a certain built-in "safety" for a practitioner. Anything you *restimulate* by *Self-determinism* is *your thing*. It is not triggered or incited by some external "*other-determined*" influences (or other "source-points" in existence) that make you an *effect*. It can be more easily handled in *processing*—or you can simply let things "cool down" and come back to it again in another *session*.

While it may seem "mysterious" to beginners, a *Seeker* gets a sense for knowing how long to *run* a *process* only with practice.

Once you have spent some time actually applying material from "*The Pathway to Ascension*" *Professional Course*, there are many aspects of it that become "second nature" because they are, in fact, a part of our true original native nature. All we have done in *Systemology* is "*reverse engineer*" the routes of *creation* and *consideration* that are already *our own*.

SYSTEMOLOGY
BIOFEEDBACK
(THE MANUAL)

"AHA, A LOOKING GLASS INTO
THE UNCONSCIOUS!"
—*Carl G. Jung*
about GSR-Meters

THE SYSTEMOLOGY OF
GSR-BIOFEEDBACK
(A SUMMARY)

This manual is restricted to students using: *The Systemology Professional Course*
and/or *The Advanced Training Course*. It is
not a matter of secrecy, but rather, proper
understanding. This manual is a supplement that *advances* other material given in
the aforementioned lessons. Its intended
meaning and usage is not likely to be
fully realized without prior experience in
our methods of *systematic processing*.

Biofeedback Systemology is only introduced
to a *Seeker* after completing *Systemology
Level-4* (of the *Professional Course* material)
at minimum. It is better for a *Solo-Pilot* to
have experience with all basic *processing*
first *without* using any *Biofeedback devices*.
These are used to "*clear up*" *lower-level*
"residual," but mainly for *advanced* work.

Traditional Piloting often includes some *Biofeedback metering device* as a tool for increasing a *Pilot's* ability to clearly indicate a *Seeker's* areas of *fragmentation* during *processing.* In this wise, such *devices* might effectively apply to *all processing-levels.*

For *Solo-Pilots*, the most significant applications for *Biofeedback devices* pertain to *Systemology Level-5* and above.

Let us begin with a quick summary of the most applicable basics. The remainder of this manual will cover more information in detail.

During the early development and practice of *"psychotherapy," Carl Jung* realized that measurable *"electrical resistance"* in the *Human Body* responded automatically to *"mental reactions"* (regarding, for example, specific *questions* or *words*). This is called *"galvanic skin response"* (or "GSR"), because this response is detected with a *"galvanometer"* — or *"Ohm-meter."*

GSR technology may be used to detect changes in the *"electrical resistance"* on the surface of the skin. But these changes are so small that a standard *"ohmmeter"* (as an electrician might use) is not functional for our purposes. The total "range" that a standard meter covers on its dial is too large—and usually has no adjustment for "sensitivity" or other "calibration."

Jung's early research led to two main applications: one being integrated into traditional *"polygraph"* equipment (which is to say, the *"lie detector"*); and the other being developed for *spiritual defragmentation* practices and *"mental health"* studies. Including *Jung*, it has a long history of usage among *New Thought* practitioners.

In physics, *electrical resistance* is measured in *"ohms."* When *fragmentation* is not in *restimulation*, the *Human Body* generally registers between *5,000* and *12,500 ohms.* This is an ideal range to be within at the start of a session for *Advanced Processing*.

Just as additional *"mass"* or *"matter"* can more greatly *"block," "restrict,"* or *"resist"* a *current* or *flow,* so too with *"resistance"* on an *"electrical circuit."* The greater the *"mental mass"* in *restimulation,* the greater the *electrical resistance* "read" on a *meter.*

A *"meter read"* of *25,000* to *60,000 ohms* might indicate the presence of *"charged fragmentation"* presently active (or *restimulated*) in a *Seeker's "Personal Universe"* — and this impinges on, or *affects,* the *Human Body* in detectable ways. A sudden "surge" up into this area can also occur when a *process* has been *"overrun"* (used past the point of *defragmentation* or when whatever was targeted got handled). This is usually remedied by *"Spotting"* the moment the actual *"relief"* or *"release"* point had occurred and *recognizing* it as such.

Visible *reactions* displayed by a *GSR-Meter* "needle" reflect the moment-to-moment *reactions* occurring with a *Seeker* during *processing.* This is important for exploring the *"almost knowns"* that remain "out-of-sight," but are *accessible.*

Biofeedback meters do not "read" (*react*) on *data* that is still "deeply buried" (and/or which a *Seeker* has *no* present-time *"reality"* on). *Systematic Processing* is intended to "uncover" what is only "partially hidden" in order to bring more "deeply hidden" data into a range accessibility. The "reads" for *"almost knowns"* are instantaneous, because a *Seeker* isn't using *"mental circuitry"* to *think* about these *things;* any *energetic-charge* detected in this range is purely *reactive.*

Several *GSR-Biofeedback* applications are mentioned within previous course materials and volumes of the *Systemology Core.* It does, however, require having not only the *equipment*, but also an *understanding* and practical *experience,* for any effective use. This manual can only help provide the *understanding*, leaving the other components for a *Seeker* to acquire.

Some of our research to support application of *GSR-Biofeedback* to *systematic processing* included:

Jung, Carl: "*Studies in Word Analysis*"

Mathison, Volney: "*Manual of Electropsychometry*" (1951)

Mathison, Volney: "*Super-Visualization: The Duplicative Techniques of Applied Creative Energy*" (1956)

Gallert, Mark: "*Electropsychometry: A New, More Effective and Faster Psychotherapy*" (1955)

Shepherd, Peter: "*GSR-Meter Course: Biofeedback Monitoring Skills in the Context of Transformational Psychotherapy*"

Khazan, Inna: "*Biofeedback & Mindfulness in Everyday Life: Practical Solutions for Improving Your Health & Performance*"

Apter, Michael: "*Reversal Theory*" and "*Personality Dynamics*"

Gerbode, Frank: "*Beyond Psychology: Traumatic Incident Reduction*"

THE HISTORY & DEVELOPMENT OF GSR-BIOFEEDBACK METERING

Experimental use of *"Psycho-Galvanometers"* (or *GSR-Meters*) for "transpersonal psychology" is as old as "psychology" and "psychoanalysis" itself. That the surface of skin is *electrically conductive*—and that *detectable resistance changes* occur from *emotional stimulation*—dates back to the late 1800's. Early "word association" investigations by *Carl Jung* demonstrated measurable "arousal" or *"electro-dermal activity"* (EDA) related to the "emotional charge" maintained by an individual regarding key *words* and *concepts*.

For our purposes, a *GSR-Meter* (or *EDA-Meter*) detects *emotional fluctuation*, measures *energetic fragmentation* and monitors changes in *Awareness* whenever a *Seeker* contacts *"charged"* terminals, *imprints* or *implants* on a particular channel.

Although design improvements (transistors, amplifiers, adjustable range &tc.) expanded its potential applications after the 1930's, the basic technology of *GSR-Meters* has remained stable and relatively unchanged since experimental research of *New Thought* movements emerging during the 1950's and 1960's.

Example of a "GSR-Meter"

One (or two) *"electrodes"* (*"sensors"* or *"probes"*) are held by, or attached to, the *Body* (*genetic-vehicle*). Early meters were little more than basic *"Ohmmeters"* lacking amplifiers and range control, making them difficult to use.

Volney G. Mathison developed the first *"Electro-Psychometer"* (the GSR *"E-Meter"*) with the intention of systematically applying the technology to *defragment* the *Human Condition.* [1950, *Patent #2684670;* *"Mathison Electrometer"* —using a single electrode held in one hand.]

Development and use of *GSR-Metering* for personal development followed along these systematic premises:

• *"Matter"* is the physical appearance of *"Energy"* (ZU) as visible or detectable within the normative range of the *Human Condition.*

• *"Energy"* (ZU) is a "super-frequency"

visible (or detectable) to *Humans* as *"matter"* or else manifest as the "stuff" of *"Mental Image Pictures."*

• *"Energy"* (ZU) may be directed by the (*Alpha*)-*Spirit* or *Self*; "raised," "lowered," "released" &tc.

• Improperly directed (or misdirected) *"Energy"* (ZU), "reduced flows" and/or "stuck flows," influence emotional states, personal illness and disease.

• An individual can modify *"Energy"* (ZU) flows, by selectively redirecting and applying *attention*, intentionally (*knowingly*) duplicating "*Mental Image Patterns*" at a "conscious" level of *Awareness*.

• *"Psycho-Physical"* *Energy* (ZU) flows of the *Human Condition* register on, and may be relatively measured with, an *"Electro-Psychometer"* (GSR/EDA *"E-Meter"*).

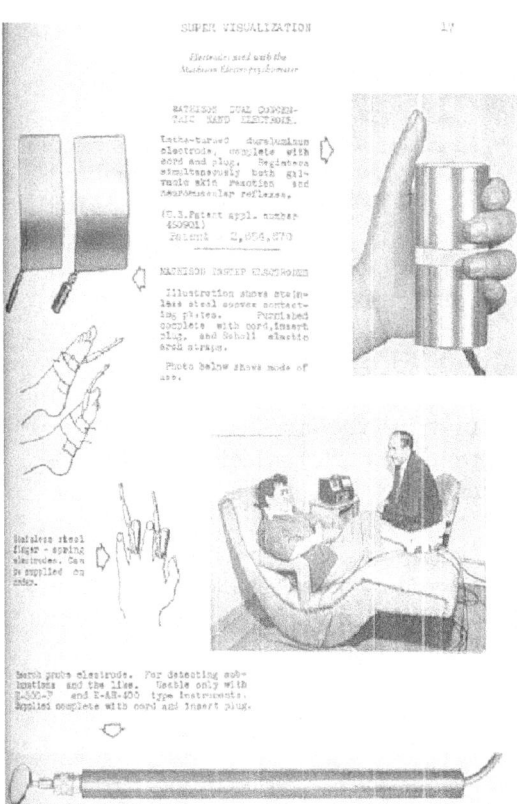

*An illustrated sample page from
Volney Mathison's "Super Visualization"*

"Volney Mathison was a pioneer in the discovery that all fears, feelings and resentments—all thought and emotion—were electrical in their nature. He found through experiments with lie-detectors during the 1940's that when a person was reminded of certain past events, or when a change of mood was induced in him, the needle in the meter would jump erratically; the degree of jump was in proportion to the strength of unconscious reaction. In skilled hands, the meter could be used to locate particular mental content, the nature of that content, the location of that content in space and time, and the amount of force contained within it."

—Peter Shepherd, *GSR Meter Course*
Tools for Transformation, 2001

Aside from "vintage" model *GSR Electro-Psychometers*, other *Biofeedback devices* that are appropriate (for our purposes) have appeared independently, with names such as: "Ability Meter" (*UK*); "Clarity Meter" (*US*); "Clearing Meter" (*generic term*); "Delta-1 Meter" (*Germany*); "Freedom-2 Meter" (*Russia*); "Mindwalker" (*UK*); and "Phoenix Meter" —just to name a few. More recent developments involve computer software. An *electrode* or *sensor* is connected to a "box" which transmits data displays to an existing device screen.

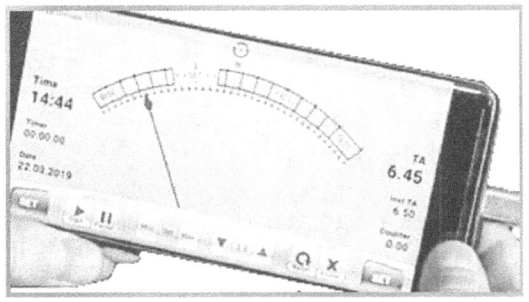

GSR technology displayed on a cell phone

Unless an individual plans to construct their own *GSR-Meter* (which is possible), the extent of "electrical" knowledge that a *Seeker* or *Pilot* needs to know is:

• Electrical *"current"* is electrical energy *"flow"*—meaning a *flow* (motion or action) of *electrons*, usually through a conductive wire; much like a *flow* of water moves through pipe or a hose.

• A "closed-loop" where *electrons* circulate (as a motion or activity) is called a *"circuit."*

• When referring to *"electrical resistance"* of a *circuit*, we quite literally mean: an *"energetic-mass"* (material) with an ability to "restrict" (slow down) *electron flow*.

• Larger or greater *electrical resistance* in a *circuit* indicates greater or denser *"mass" resisting free-flow* of *electrons* in that *circuit*.

HISTORICAL FACT

The basic electrical circuit used to measure an unknown (or variable) value of electrical resistance is called the *"Wheatstone bridge"*—named not for its original inventor (*Samuel Hunter Christie* in 1833), but for *Sir Charles Wheatstone*, an English scientist that improved and popularized its application and notoriety in 1843.

When a *Seeker* holds *electrodes* (*"sensors"*) of an *Electro-Psychometer* in their hands, they are part of a closed-circuit. A small amount of electrical current (usually no more than two volts) is passed through the *Body*, which now acts as one "leg" (or "side") of "resistance" in the circuit.

To determine the unknown value of *resistance* from the *Body*, a *"potentiometer"* (*"variable resistor"* and *"range adjuster"*) is attached to the other "leg" ("side") and is controlled externally on the device by a rotating "knob" or "arm."

This "balancing arm" (or "baseline control") is manually rotated to a position where the "display-dial needle" is visibly at the "set" point, indicating a "balance point" is reached for the circuit.

While the "needle" is at the "set" point, the circuit is balanced: the "balancing arm" (or "baseline control") position on one "leg" or "side" of the "circuit bridge" indicates the *electrical resistance ("ohms")* present across the surface of the skin on the other "leg" or "side" of the circuit.

> This is rather like using a "balancing scale" to determine the weight of something by adding a known amount (quantity/value/weight) to the other side.

All *GSR-Biofeedback devices* measure resistance, but may not display data in *ohms*.

On Mathison's original models, arbitrary "number values" were assigned to the "balancing arm" for simplification, rather than use large *ohms* values. There was still a preassigned relationship between the two values. The following is only an example of this.

Balancing Arm	Resistance
1	500 Ω
2	5000 Ω
3	12,500 Ω
4	25,000 Ω
5	60,000 Ω
6	180,000 Ω

Standard *ohmmeters* feature display-dials covering such a large range that we don't see precise movements. *GSR-Meters* allow an individual to display a smaller portion (or range) of what the visible dial represents—and most have controls to increase or decrease amplification (sensitivity).

"It is a remarkable fact that the real sources of one's anxiety may be so deeply hidden in one's subconscious that one will go about believing all sorts of other things are causing all the trouble, and erroneously blaming these other things which are *secondary effects*, not *causes*. Meanwhile, the *true cause* remains hidden, growing ever more powerful in its own *effects.*"

—V. Mathison, <u>Super-Visualization</u>
Manual of Electropsychometry, 1956

"When restimulated mental content is confronted, repression dissolves into *Awareness*. When not *confronted*, detachment may suffice, but if further involvement is enforced or encountered, then anxiety results."

—Peter Shepherd, <u>GSR Meter Course</u>
Tools for Transformation, 1994-2001

UNDERSTANDING GSR-BIOFEEDBACK
FOR SPIRITUAL DEFRAGMENTATION

Prior to *Carl Jung's* incorporation of *GSR-Meters* for 'Word Association', the standard gauge of "psychoanalytics" primarily consisted of observing "*comm-lag*" (or *communication lag*); which is the amount of time it takes an individual to directly answer a question.

The intended purpose of *Systematic Processing* is to bring undesirable, implanted and artificial *programs, imprints* and *postulates* into clear view for a *Seeker* to analytically inspect "*As-It-Is.*"

Suppressed *fragmentation, imprints* and *programming* are uncovered in layers—as some is taken off, more becomes accessible that previously might not even register on the *Meter*. This is elevation of *Actualized Awareness* in action and objectively on display to measure.

An individual that avoids "handling their stuff" runs the risk of having the *charge* restimulated by their environment in everyday life. Energy-flows encounter resistance from *mass*, just like damming up a stream of water. Hence, in most cases, the higher the resistance, the greater the *mass* encountered. Here we mean quite specifically and literally *"mental mass"* (or *"fields"*) surrounding certain 'ideas' and 'concepts'—or as *Carl Jung* was researching, associated with certain 'words' and 'memories'.

> As *energetically-entangled mental masses* are brought up to the "surface" for a *Seeker* to *confront*, the *resistance* may increase—or *"rise."* When the *mass* is actually *confronted As-It-Is* and disintegrated with the *Seeker's* "attention energy"—or else *"Actualized Awareness"*—then the *Meter* reads a *resistance* reduction, or *"fall."*

The device is not a substitute for understanding. A *Seeker* would already have to be familiar with vocabulary and concepts applied to a *process* or PCL. For example: a misunderstood word given in a *process* can cause false readings. Therefore, it is important to check each actual word used in a PCL prior to applying them, in order to be certain they do not already have a "*charge*" on them. This goes back to the original *Jungian* application of GSR for 'word association'.

A *GSR-Meter* is particularly useful when *Piloting* a *Seeker*. Although it does not indicate exactly *what* the *Seeker* is thinking about or confronting, it can indicate shifts in attention and *how* the *Seeker* is handling it.

Meters don't necessarily "read" the *Mind* —but they do register how the *Mind-System* is affecting the *Body* as it operates. For example: by observing the *Seeker* and

GSR-Meter, a *Pilot* can determine when a *"hot-button"* is 'pressed' or *contacted* during *processing*—or when the *Seeker* is *withdrawing* (backing off) from the same.

There are indications for when the *Seeker* is experiencing *restimulation* of an *Imprint* —and also for when there is no longer a *"charge"* of entangled energy remaining on a particular circuit or channel.

The *Meters* are intended only as *tools* to assist *systematic processing* and should not be the ultimate focus. A *Pilot* is *processing* the *Seeker;* not the *Meter device* itself. It is also not a substitute for observing reactions and behaviors of a *Seeker.*

While it is true that excessively sweaty, cold or dry hands can affect the baseline read from the *electrodes* (and should be remedied before a *systematic session* begins), use of a *GSR-Meter* (as we describe and apply it) does not have anything to do with *"perspiration"*—which is what many skeptics and critics suggest. A *Human Body* does not sweat and "un-sweat" rapidly enough to provide the kind of instant *reactive reads* and changes we look for and observe during *systematic* use. By *reactive read*, we mean literally within an instant or second of a *Pilot* completing a statement, word or PCL. Anything more than three seconds and you are dealing with latent surface thought.

There are *Biofeedback* or *GSR-devices* on the market that do not possess the same features as the *Meters* described in this manual. Many of them should not really be called "*Meters.*" They act more like "monitors," similar to a smoke detector. But those sold as "meditation trainers" or "stress-relaxation aids" likely resulted from a completely different type of experimental research than our own. That is not to say that this area does not require and deserve more research. A *Seeker* may find ways that they *can* be used.

In *processing sessions*, we are most interested in times when a *GSR-Meter* indicates a sudden *reduction* of *resistance*—or "*fall*." This denotes something that the *Seeker* is able to handle, *reach* for and is ready to *confront*; it denotes an increase in *Awareness* applied and a *willingness* to take *responsibility* for handling it. An *increase* or "*rise*" in *resistance* would indicate the opposite of this.

Of course, in order to have "*falls*" during a session there must be points when the *Meter* reads a rise—or that the Balance Point is at a relatively higher resistance. But, we are talking about *processing* each individual "item" or "terminal" (or an *imprinting incident* or event).

After *charge* on a particular area or item is indicated by a "*fall*," the *needle* (*meter display*) will measure a *reduction* of *resistance* when the *Seeker* no longer resists directly handling/confronting it while *processing*.

A *Pilot* keeps an eye on the *Meter* to determine that a question or item is *"reading"* (causing a "change" on the *Meter*) before it is *systematically processed*. If it doesn't *"read"* then it isn't taken up in *processing* at that time.

Processing a *"charged"* terminal or incident continues so long as there is still a *"read"* (change) taking place. If there was no indicator (or *"read"*) to begin with, there would be no real way to gauge this; there would be no way to determine when a *Seeker* had effectively flattened that *wave-action* (or energetic *"ridge"*).

A *"ridge"* is perhaps one of the most *solid-state* "waveform patterns" encountered when an individual is working with *energies*. It is essentially an *"energetic-mass"* formed from two opposing *energy-wave flows*. In some ways, all physical *"matter"* could be considered a highly condensed and compacted energetic *"ridge."*

But rather than dissolving solid physical matter, we are concerned with *flattening* the "solidity" of "*collapsed wave-functions*" that form and collect as "*energetic-masses*" all around one's own *Personal Universe*. [See *Lesson-16* of the *Professional Course*.]

The "stuck" *Mental Image Pictures* and "reactive" *imprinting* are formed on-and-as such "ridges." And they have a tendency to build up into greater and greater "*masses*" when left improperly handled.

> When a *Seeker* is truly able and *willing* to handle, manage and/or *confront* the nature of their "stuff" *As-It-Is*, that increased *Awareness* is enough to "blow" the *fragmentation* apart.

A common experiment is to learn the "yes"/"no" *Meter*-reads and reactions by working with a list of questions (or generating them at the time) for which there is no mystery about the answers. For example: Are you sitting down? Are we presently inside/outside? Do you drive a car/have a license to drive a car? But nothing that digs to deep under the surface.

To get further practice and experience with what is taking place when using a *Meter* in session (and for handling *Ethics* or other *Integrity Checkups*), you can instruct a *Seeker* or partner to intentionally "lie" about an answer to a question that is otherwise obvious. For example: if they are sitting down—or if they are indoors—have them answer that they are not to each and see what and how things *"read."*

"When [a mass or '*ridge*'] is restimulated by events or in session—if the material is too hard to experience or confront, it is repressed and there will not be an instantaneous response on the meter. The *ridge* will remain in restimulation but out of consciousness, until attention is directed to the item and it is confronted. This is a flight away from the *ridge.* If the client is able to view it, some of the suppressed emotional charge is released, causing a *fall* in resistance. This happens instantly. However, mental defenses may kick-in causing a backing off or resistance to the contents, because it may be hard to face. This stops the release of charge and the resistance may *rise*—still accessible but the client is fighting against it. A *rise*, then, relates to content that is being confronted, but is also fought against.

—Peter Shepherd, <u>GSR Meter Course</u>
Tools for Transformation, 2001

UNDERSTANDING GSR-METERS
& HOW TO READ THEM

When working with a *GSR-Meter* for *systematic processing*, the most common term is *"read"*—like when you hear someone say, "that *reads*." More often than not it indicates a decrease in resistance or *"fall."*

There are also rare instances where the *Meter*, or more accurately, the observed *needle*, doesn't *read* anything at all for anything no matter what you do. The term *"stuck needle"* is often applied here, meaning that a *Seeker* is not offering their presence to the session. There is likely a break in *communication* (or a *"flow-factor"* as described in the *Professional Course*).

It is important to know whether or not a reaction is going to read, otherwise it gives an illusion that there is no *"charge"* on something, which may now be blown over—or *flown* over—when it should be handled. Operating a *session* in this way, when a *Seeker* is not providing presence, will actually reduce a *Seeker's* participation even further. The session, methods and *Pilot* lose credibility—even at "subconscious" levels; even when the *Seeker* is the one causing, allowing or validating the break in attention themselves.

So long as the sensitivity is kept constant then the *reads* on a *Meter* may be compared to other *reads*. For the "*falls*" you would be looking for the "largest" read or "*largest fall*" in relation to other *reads*. This is important when you are seeking to scout out a particular answer among variables.

For example: if you were to ask a *Seeker* which of their former jobs contributed to the most fragmentation, there may be some "*charge*" on more than one answer; therefore you are looking for the biggest reaction or *read* when each is named.

We often use the term *"resurfacing"* to denote bringing something into view that was hidden "beneath-the-surface." The quicker the response from a *Meter*, the closer something is to the "surface."

If something doesn't *read*, a *Pilot* should avoid focusing further attention on it. Of course, this does not mean that the *channel* is clear or there is no energetic *charge* held on the terminal in question—but it is not presently accessible or within the *Seeker's* reach or tolerance level to confront at that given time.

Without a *read*, there is no guarantee a *Pilot* can determine full erasure of that *fragmentation* or an *End Point*. This is what we mean about continuing a particular *process* or area of work so long as it is producing a change in *Awareness*; but not to a point of being *overrun*.

Using a *GSR-Meter* makes it a little easier for a *Pilot* to determine if an *End Point* is reached. It is critical to fully eliminate re-active "*charge*" from anything that either does *resurface*, or that can be made to *re-surface*, so long as it is *reading* on the Meter. If a *Pilot* doesn't treat a *process* through to finality, then the "*Universe*" (*society, &tc.*) will most certainly keep "*running* it" and the *Seeker* will become increasingly withdrawn.

To establish a systematic standard for re-cording a *session*, we have established a chart for *Systemology* that applies to many *GSR-Meter* models used for spiritual de-fragmentation. On such models, the dial-display has a 90-degree range—showing a quarter of a circle. As illustrated, there is a *9-centimeter* arc of potential motion: *one centimeter* per *ten-degrees*.

In most cases, the area given to read the "*falls*" constitutes half of the *Meter*. It is the differences between reactions in this zone that are of primary interest for the session and its records.

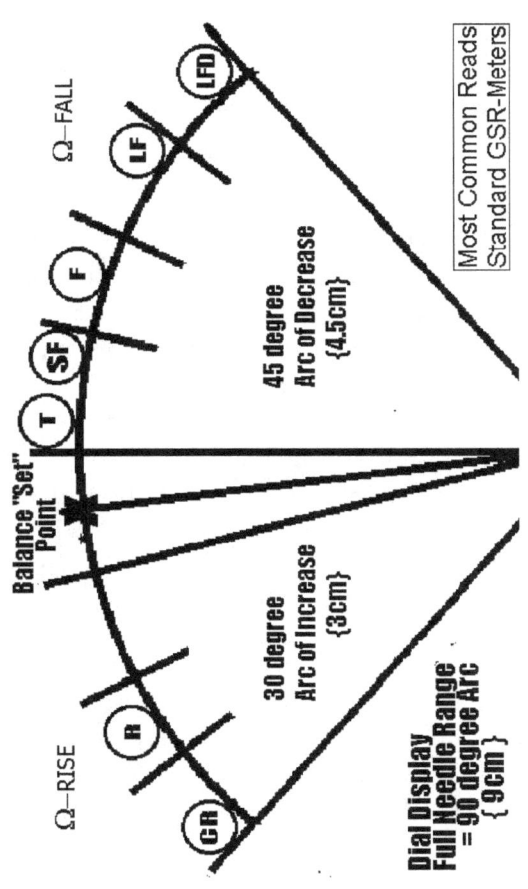

Ω–FALL

Ω–RISE

Balance "Set" Point

45 degree
Arc of Decrease
{4.5cm}

30 degree
Arc of Increase
{3cm}

Dial Display
Full Needle Range
= 90 degree Arc
{ 9cm }

Most Common Reads
Standard GSR-Meters

T SF F LF LFD

R GR

Although not all practitioners with prior experience (using this type of technology) have the same interpretation for *reads*, using our chart offers the greatest stability or consistency in what we are looking for.

The Balance-Point or Set-Point provides a BASELINE reading and it reflects the basic state of a *Seeker* when at "rest" (presently in the session), without being aroused or directly *restimulated* by internal thought or the environment, *&tc*. A *read* is then taken when the needle moves off of, or out of, the small 15-degree region given for this. Sometimes a TINY TICK is *read* within this region; but if all session activity remains so close to the Balance-Point, it may be that the sensitivity is too low.

The answer to *"does it read?"* (hypothetical) could also be considered an answer to whatever "YES/NO" question you pose as a PCL. Therefore a *read* typically means "YES" or "there is something there."

The *Physical Universe* is solidified by com-pacted matter that philosophically are "lies." When an individual is confronting (facing up to) the truth about something, they are practically disintegrating its ef-fects on one's *Personal Universe*. Hence you get a reduced *mass* and reduced *res-istance* ("*fall*"). Therefore, it is possible to get an increase-decrease fluctuation dur-ing a single *process*.

When a PCL or "item" results in a FALL, it means there is some degree of energetic "*charge*" available for a *Seeker* to *confront*. But then they could find while examining it, that they suddenly feel "resistive" to it, which literally adds "*resistance*" demonstrated by a RISE.

However, if a *Seeker* overcomes this withdrawal and continues to *confront* it, you will continue to see a FALL (usually a "LARGE/LONG FALL"/"LF") until it significantly "BALANCE DROPS" (requiring movement of the *Balancing-Arm* to keep the *needle* "balanced" on the *Meter dial-display*). Since this *read* is a LARGE/LONG FALL and a (BALANCE) DROP it is often written/recorded "LFD" or LFBD.

The basic *reads,* as they appear marked on our previous chart, are as follows:

(R) RISE (R)

Any movement of the needle on the left side of the "Set Point" (BA); no additional differentiation is made—unless it is a "Continuous Rise" (CR)—just the fact that the needle and resistance is *rising* (has *risen*). If it never did this you would not get any "*Balance-Arm* action" in *processing*. An initial increase in resistance to a question means literally increased resistance *to* the question; it can *fall* once a *Seeker* permits themselves to confront it *As-It-Is.*

Since a *rise* generally indicates a *Seeker* does not want to confront what has been presented, it is best *not* to announce this *read* when it occurs. If pressed further in that direction the *Seeker* will break with *reality flow-factors* and *communication* and potentially go "out of session."

(CR) CONTINUOUS RISE (CR)

A large enough *rise* to the left side of the meter that requires the Balance-Arm to be adjusted to keep the needle within range of the dial-display. A question that immediately stops a "rising needle" is a change in characteristics and should be considered the same as a *Fall*.

Sessions where the *reads* do not seem to be coming as expected may require monitoring for any change in characteristics rather than other *reads*. So, if the needle is continuously *rising* but a question stops its motion—or it has been doing nothing but then decides to dance—this is a change in characteristics.

(BA)/(BP) BALANCE-ARM SET POINT (BA)/(BP)

The reading taken when the armature fixes the needle on the set point (or at least in the balanced range). If *Low* BA/BP—is below "2.0" (5000 *ohms*)—exceptionally decreased resistance possibly hyper-vigilant or overwhelmed; If *High* BA/BP—above "4.5" (35,000 *ohms*)—increased resistance is possibly withdrawal, dissociation and/or detachment.

If the BA/BP is *High* at the start of the session, the *Seeker's* attention is already directed on some "mass" elsewhere. You can start to free up these attention units by two-way communication with the *Seeker* about "where" their attention is.

"Do you have your attention on anything?" "Is there anything you would like to tell me?" "Since your last session, is there anything that has happened?"

A Seeker is not trained in "solo-metering" for lower *processing-levels*. However, when combining two electrodes with a coupler—making certain the two do not touch—to hold in one hand, the BA/BP will be higher than standard (by a factor of as much as "0.5" higher) reads. Therefore what might be "2.1" (5500 *ohms*) when each electrode is held in its own hand, would then potentially be around "2.6" (9000 *ohms*) when *soloing* with one hand.

(X) NO/NULL READ (X)

As the name suggests, there is no read and the needle remains at rest at the "Set Point" (BA). "No charge" or an answer of "no" should be distinguishable from a "stuck needle" based on characteristics of meter reads throughout the *session* up to this point or from a proper *session* setup that guarantees the *Seeker* is participating or has presence in *session*.

(T) TICK/TINY READ (T)

A rapid *fall* of less than a few millimeters to the right of the "Set Point" (BA); as the name suggests, it barely counts as read. It may or may not even leave the "Balanced Range." If you get a small "trace read" from a question, trying varying the wording. If the same small "tick" or "tiny read" is all that occurs after three inquiries, move on.

(SF) SMALL/SHORT FALL (SF)

Up to one centimeter (or ½ an inch) *fall* to the right side of the "Set Point" (BA). Any amount of *fall* is still a *fall;* if you are still getting a *read* after several runs or exhausted question/answer, the *Seeker* still "hasn't told all" or else you are dealing with a "past life" or an area they do not "consciously know about."

If a decent *read* occurs when the *Seeker* hasn't said anything, inquire about it. "What was that there?" "What did you just think of there?" "Did you have a thought there?"

(F) FALL (F)

One to two centimeters (½ inch to one inch) *fall* to the right side of the "Set Point" (BA). Any length of *fall* is a standard *read* or "Yes" answer to your question; for some techniques (*processes*) the largest/longest *fall*-read is the answer.

(LF) LARGE/LONG FALL (LF)

Two to six centimeters (1 to 3 inches) *fall* to the right side of the "Set Point" (BA). Among several possible *reads*, the largest/longest *read* or *fall* is the answer.

(LFD/LFBD) LARGE/LONG FALL BALANCE DROP

A large enough *fall* to the right side of the meter that requires the Balance-Arm to be adjusted to keep the needle within range of the dial-display. A massive discharge of this caliber accompanies the *Seeker* having confronted (faced-up-to) or seeing (knowingly duplicating creation of) something *As-It-Is*, thereby duplicating and eradicating what and where something is by consciously placing one's own there—seeing it for what *It Is* on one's own volition.

"If the [*Seeker*] knew about the subconscious reactive contents of the mind, they wouldn't be subconscious or reactive. But the *GSR-Meter* responds to the reactive emotional charge. Hence, you don't follow up something unless it gives a read. You don't let the [*Seeker's*] analytical (cognitive) mind control the session or give it free reign to talk about anything it likes. It is a [*Pilot's*] responsibility to control the session. The [*Pilot*] has more control over the [*Seeker's*] case, since the [*Seeker*] is influenced by the case."

—Peter Shepherd, <u>GSR Meter Course</u>
Tools for Transformation, 2001

APPLYING GSR-METERS TO SYSTEMATIC PROCESSING

This course supplement has provided a tremendous amount of basic fundamentals regarding history, purposes and usage of *GSR-Biofeedback Meters*. Volney Mathison's own publication (*"Super-Visualization"*) includes a basic *"session script"* that offers examples of what might be expected when applying *GSR-Meters* to methods similar to our own presentation of *systematic processing* in previous lessons.

Use of a *Meter* does not in itself solve the matter of getting the *Seeker* to participate *presence* in *sessions*, with attention fully on *processing*; there are no substitutes for skillfully *Piloting* a *Seeker*—it must be learned and practiced. This includes actual certainty on handling a *Meter* when it is applied to *processing*; and this is best gained only by experience.

Having the *Seeker* "squeeze the cans" (and then release) is a popular way of setting/adjusting the *sensitivity* before a *session* really begins. Intentional "squeezes" should only produce a one-inch *fall.* The device can be adjusted for this. It also shows the difference between an actual *"read"* versus simply adding *"pressure."*

Once a *process* has begun, it is best if the *sensitivity* does not have to be readjusted. When you are rapidly comparing relative "lengths" of various *falls,* the *sensitivity* must remain constant. There are some instances (especially in *Ethics Processing* for *Personal Integrity*) when you really want to see if a question is getting a solid *read* or not. You can always raise the *sensitivity* for that particular PCL, but make sure to return it to where it was afterward.

If everything that you are asking or saying is getting large reads, you may need to turn the *sensitivity* down. A simple determinant of basic stress levels can be observed at the beginning of a *session* to check this. Simply ask: *"How are you going to feel about my asking you a lot of personal questions?"*

Of course, we are not really concerned about a *Seeker's* answer, so much as what kind of *read* is observed. If there is a strong *read* in response to this, it is likely that the *Seeker* has experienced uncomfortable interrogation in the past, either from a family member or some other source. It is helpful if communication can be used between the *Pilot* and *Seeker* to quiet these *reads* before proceeding. This occurs simply by identifying the underlying source of the *turbulence*.

If a *Seeker's* attention is not directed precisely on the session and PCL, there is no way to determine what the *reads* on a *Meter* actually pertain to. Having the *Seeker* acknowledge the *Pilot*—a reality on the fact that the *Pilot* is the *Pilot*—is quite critical for the *Pilot* being able to get (and keep) the *Seeker in-session*.

There is at least one key reason why this is sometimes difficult—and this can be checked with the *Meter* prior to a true session start. *Pilot* asks: "*Do I remind you in some way of a person you have known whom you feared or disliked?*"

If there is no *read* on that, or if there is only a *tiny tick*, consider rephrasing the PCL slightly: "*Is there anything about me that is similar to some person that bothered or injured you in the past?*" If any of these types of questions indicates a YES, then *defragment* that line using basic communication regarding the underlying issue. Resolving things like this is, of course, critical for success; but it also directly facilitates getting the *Seeker* to participate with *presence* in the *session*.

"A sharp prolonged meter surge on 'How do you feel about your name?' indicates one of two things: the (Seeker) is using a false, an assumed, or an altered name—or—more commonly, the (Seeker) dislikes their name for some specific reason which they can readily clarify. A disliked name has some unpleasant or silly connotation or association. Sometimes a name is changed to forget a hated parent, a past mate, or the like. Meter surges on such situations are all significant and should be discussed until tension on them subsides. Laughter, yawns and sighs will cause major needle surges, owing to flash metabolic effects, and may, in general, be disregarded. Do not permit the (Seeker) to tap on the electrode with finger or thumb. Minor needle surges may merely indicate mental activity. Major surges indicate areas of pain or tension."

—Volney Mathison, *Super-Visualization Manual of Electropsychometry, 1956*

As a chiropractor, Mathison's initial interests for using an *"Electro-psychometer"* pertained to the physiological body long before concepts of *spiritual defragmentation* became paramount. Therefore, in his manual—prior to the *Test Questionnaire* (given hereafter)—he describes a progressive *'Deep Meditation' technique* that is otherwise very similar to *'Energetic Body Scanning'*.

For example: a *Pilot* gives the PCL: "Toes, left foot, relax." [Or, alternatively to "relax": "Let go" or "Let go of the tension."]

The *Seeker* would then silently deliver the PCL/message to the *Body* (*genetic vehicle*) and report back with "Okay" after having done so. The *Pilot* closes that communication cycle with an acknowledgment (*"Thank You"*) and begins the next cycle: *"Now, ankle, left foot, relax."* And onward in this fashion, treating each portion of the *Body*.

If at any point the *Pilot* sees a "sharp needle surge" on the *Meter* in relation to a certain part of the body, nothing is said, but a notation is made. Once a list of all *Body* areas is completed, the *Pilot* returns to those which were indicated and if the unrest still persists, additional *attention* is given to them with the PCL: *"Be at ease."*

Here is the original *Test Questionnaire* that appears in Mathison's *Electropsychometry Manual* (from 1956). Strong *reads* or "surges" (as he calls them) should be reduced with *processing* and *communication* (techniques described in the *Professional Course*). As an "assessment," this is really meant to "open a case" and not necessarily "solve" every aspect of a *Seeker's* life. It allows a *Pilot* to get a general idea of where some significant trouble-spots are. An attempt should be made, however, to reduce the *"charge"* on anything found to give major *reads* before continuing on with other standard *processing-levels*.

MATHISON'S QUESTIONNAIRE

1. How do you feel about your name?

2. What is your occupation? How do you feel about it?

3. How do you feel about your mother? About your father?

4. What sort of person do you fear? Hate?

5. Mention one of the worst things that has happened to you.

6. What do you think of a person that commits suicide? [*A heavy surge may indicate a suicide risk or that they a Seeker has lost someone close this way.*]

7. Have you ever been in a hospital?

8. Have you ever been injured in an accident?

9. Whom did you hate or fear most when you were a child?

10. Mention some things you are very anxious about or that you feel should not occur. Mention some things you would fight or struggle against to keep them from happening.

11. Who loves you?

12. Who used to love you, but no longer does?

13. Can you think of a time when you wished someone would love you?

14. Do you feel remorse, regret or blame over the way you have treated some person? Mother? Father? Wife? Husband? &tc.

15. If you were writing a novel and you had to depict some injurious thing happening to a baby or a child, what would have this thing be?

16. Have you ever been struck or severely beaten?

17. How do you think women feel about you?

18. How do you think men feel about you?

19. How do you think children feel about you?

20. Have you ever been through an unhappy love experience?

21. Do you love your wife/husband? [*This is asked without the mate present.*]

22. How do you think your wife/husband feels about you?

23. Have you ever been attacked or severely shocked sexually? [*It may not be advisable to explore this content directly; particularly if the Seeker and Pilot are unfamiliar to each other and/or of different genders.*]

24. Are you presently satisfied with your sexual activities?

25. Have you ever had a bitter quarrel with a man? Woman? Mention actual incidents.

26. What do you think about the use of contraceptives? Abortions?

27. What do you think about illegitimate children?

28. What do you think of a woman who is frigid? Or a man who is impotent?

29. What do you think of a sexual sadist? Masochist?

30. Have you ever been jeered at, made fun of, or painfully rejected?

31. What things do you keep doing that you wish you didn't do?

32. What changes do you wish to make in yourself?

33. Mention three goals or ambitions that you have wished to achieve—and which you have achieved.

34. Mention three goals or ambitions that you have wished to achieve—and which you have not achieved.

ADVANCED APPLICATIONS &
THE PROFESSIONAL COURSE

In *Traditional Piloting*, if a *Seeker* slows or stalls on the *Pathway*, it is up to the *Pilot* to determine why. Of course, really it is only the *Seeker*, themselves, that knows— even if they don't think that it is the reason why. But, it is still a *Pilot's* responsibility to discover it for all concerned, and often this involves probing various areas directly (often with assistance of an *GSR-biofeedback device*). In *Solo-Piloting*, a *Seeker* must discover, *identify* and *confront* the underlying fundamental *breaks, upsets,* and *fragmentation*, themselves, with or without assistance of a *GSR-Meter*.

Starting with *Systemology Level-5* (*Lesson-11* of the *Professional Course*), a *Seeker* begins dealing more with "*things*" (*terminals* and *forms*) and "*incidents*" that are not directly encountered (or typically visible) from within the normative "confines" or "limitations" of the *Human Condition*. Although they continue to affect our experience of *Beta-Existence*, they "perturb" and "impinge" upon our *reality* as an "unseen source" of various creations, personal reactivity and manifestations in our *Personal Universe*.

Biofeedback devices may be used to detect when *fragmented charge* in certain "unseen areas" is present. So, what we are speaking of is not entirely "undetectable," just not always *knowingly* sensed, especially if it is presently "active" or "*restimulated.*"

Some basic techniques for "*defragmenting implants*" (for *advanced processing*) are given in the *Professional Course*. For *Level-5*, without a meter, the basic procedure is:

A. "*Spot (or Imagine) an implant-item (or command-item in the listed sequence).*"

B. "*Confront it until it ceases to have any effect.*"

The easiest way for a *Seeker* to accomplish this is to alternately:

A. *"Spot the implanted command-item."*
B. *"Spot something in the room."*

"Command-Items" are/were not *implanted* in "English" (or any language of Human speech). Therefore, the best we can do for *processing* is to *"approximate"* their meaning (*get a sense* for their original *intention*) when each *"command-item"* is *"Spotted."*

When a *GSR-Meter* is applied to this practice, then *"Step-B"* is technically replaced with *"Spotting the Meter display for reads."*

A *Seeker* *"Spots"* the *"item"* on a certain list and then immediately checks the *Meter* for a *"read."* This continues, alternating *attention* between the "item" and the *Meter* until no *"charge"* is *reading.* A *Seeker* *"runs"* this *process* on each "item" given on the list. This same method applies to *processing-out* other *considerations.*

GLOSSARY

actualization : to make actual, not just potential; to bring into full solid Reality; to realize fully in *Awareness* as a "thing."

agreement (reality) : unanimity of opinion of what is "thought" to be known; an accepted arrangement of how things are; things we consider as "real" or as an "is" of "reality"; a consensus of what is real as made by standard-issue (common) participants; what an individual contributes to or accepts as "real"; in *Systemology*, a synonym for "*reality*."

alpha : the first, primary, basic, superior or beginning of some form; in *Systemology*, referring to the state of existence operating on spiritual archetypes and postulates, will and intention "exterior" to the low-level condensation and solidarity of energy and matter as the 'physical universe' (*beta*).

alpha-spirit : a "spiritual" *Life*-form; the "true" *Self* or I-AM; the *individual*; the spiritual (*alpha*) *Self* that is animating the (*beta*) physical body or "*genetic vehicle*" using a continuous *Lifeline* of spiritual ("*ZU*") energy; an individual spiritual (*alpha*) entity possessing no physical mass or measurable waveform (motion) in the Physical Universe as itself, so it animates the (*beta*) physical body or "*genetic vehicle*" as a catalyst to experience *Self*-determined causality in effect within the *Physical Universe*; a singular unit or point of *Spiritual Awareness* that is *Aware* that it is *Aware*.

alpha thought : the highest spiritual *Self-determination* over creation and existence exercised by an Alpha-Spirit; the Alpha range of pure *Creative Ability* based on direct postulates and considerations of *Beingness*; spiritual qualities comparable to "thought" but originating in Alpha-existence, independently superior to a Mind-System.

ascension : actualized *Awareness* elevated to the point of true "spiritual existence" exterior to *beta existence*. An "Ascended Master" is one who has returned to an incarnation on Earth as an inherently *Enlightened One*, demonstrable in their words and actions; they have the ability to *Self-direct* the "Mind" and "Body" as *Self* (as a "Spirit"); and to maintain consciousness as a personal identity continuum with the same *Self-directed* control and communication of Will-Intention that is exercised, actualized and developed deliberately during one's present incarnation.

associative knowledge : significance or meaning of a facet or aspect assigned to (or considered to have) a direct relationship with another facet; to connect or relate ideas or facets of existence with one another; in traditional systems logic, an equivalency of significance or meaning between facets or sets that are grouped together, such as in *(a + b) + c = a + (b + c)*; in Systemology, erroneous associative knowledge is assignment of the same value to all facets or parts considered as related (even when they are not actually so), such as in *a = a, b = a, c = a* and so forth without distinction.

attention : active use of *Awareness* toward a specific aspect or thing; the act of "attending" with the presence of *Self*; a direction of focus or concentration of *Awareness* along a particular channel or conduit or toward a particular terminal node or communication termination point; the Self-directed concentration of personal energy as a combination of observation, thought-waves and consideration; focused application of *Self-Directed Awareness*.

awareness : the highest sense of-and-as *Self* in knowing and being as I-AM (the *Alpha-Spirit*); the extent of beingness directed as a viewpoint (POV) experienced by *Self* as *Knowingness*.

beta (awareness) : all consciousness activity ("*Awareness*") in the "Physical Universe" (KI, in *Zuism*) or else in *beta-existence*; *Awareness* within the range of the *genetic-body*, including material thoughts, emotional responses and physical motors; personal *Awareness* of physical energy and physical matter moving through physical space and experienced as "time"; the *Awareness* held by *Self* that is restricted to an organic *Lifeform* or "*genetic vehicle*" in which it experiences causality in *beta-existence*.

beta (existence) : all manifestation in the "Physical Universe" (KI, in *Zuism*); the conditions of *Awareness* for the *Alpha-spirit* (*Self*) as a physical organic *Lifeform* or "*genetic vehicle*" in which it experiences causality in the *Physical Universe*.

charge : to fill or furnish with a quality; to supply with energy; to lay a command upon; in *Systemology*—to imbue with intention; to overspread with emotion; personal energy stores and significances entwined as fragmentation in mental images, reactive-response encoding and intellectual (and/or) programmed beliefs.

channel : a specific stream, course, current, direction or route; to form or cut a groove or ridge or otherwise guide along a specific course; a direct path; an artificial aqueduct created to connect two water bodies or water or make travel possible.

circuit : a circular path or loop; a closed-path within a system that allows a flow; a pattern or action or wave movement that follows a specific route or potential path only; in *Systemology*, "*communication processing*" pertaining to a specific *flow* of energy or information along a channel; "*feedback loop.*"

communication : successful transmission of information, data, energy (&tc.) along a message line, with a reception of feedback; an energetic flow of intention to cause an effect (or duplication) at a distance; the personal energy moved or acted upon by will or else 'selective directed attention'; the 'messenger action' used to transmit and receive energy across a medium; also relay of energy, a message or signal—or even locating a personal POV (viewpoint) for the Self—along the *ZU-line*.

condense (condensation) : the transition of vapor to liquid; denoting a change in state to a more substantial or solid condition; leading to a more compact or solid form.

confront : to come around in front of; to be in the presence of; to stand in front of, or in the face of; to meet "face-to-face" or "face-up-to"; additionally, in *Systemology*, to fully tolerate or acceptably withstand an encounter with a particular manifestation without an automatic reactive response.

consideration : careful analytical reflection of all aspects; deliberation; determining the significance of a "thing" in relation to similarity or dissimilarity to other "things"; evaluation of facts and importance of certain facts; thorough examination of all aspects related to, or important for, making a decision; the analysis of consequences and estimation of significance when making decisions; also in *Systemology*, the *postulate* or *Alpha-Thought* that defines the state of *beingness* for what something "*is.*"

defragmentation : the *reparation* of wholeness; collecting all dispersed parts to reform an original whole; a process of removing "*fragmentation*" in data or knowledge to provide a clear understanding; applying techniques and processes that promote a *holistic* interconnected *alpha* state, favoring observational *Awareness* of continuity in all spiritual and physical systems; in *Systemology*, a "*Seeker*" achieving actualized "*Self-Honest Awareness*" is said to be in a basic state of *beta-defragmentation*, whereas *Alpha-defragmentation* is the rehabilitation of the *creative ability*, managing the *Spiritual Timeline* and the POV of *Self* as Alpha-Spirit (I-AM).

existence : the *state* or fact of *apparent manifestation*; the resulting combination of the Principles of Manifestation: consciousness, motion and substance; continued *survival*; that which independently exists.

exterior : outside of; on the outside; in *Systemology*, we mean specifically the POV of *Self* that is *'outside of'* the *Human Condition,* free of the physical and mental trappings of the Physical Universe; a metahuman range of consideration; see also *'Zu-Vision'*.

external : a force coming from outside; information received from outside sources; in *Systemology*, the objective *'Physical Universe'* existence, or *beta-existence*, that the Physical Body or *genetic vehicle* is essentially *anchored* to for its considerations of locational space-time as a dimension or POV.

fragmentation : breaking into parts and scattering the pieces; the *fractioning* of wholeness or the *fracture* of a holistic interconnected *alpha* state, favoring observational *Awareness* of perceived connectivity between parts; *discontinuity*; separation of a totality into parts; in *Systemology*, a person outside of *Self-Honesty* is said to be operating from a *fragmented* state.

flow : movement across (or through) a channel (or conduit); a direction of active energetic motion, typically distinguished as either an *in-flow*, *out-flow* or *cross-flow*.

genetic-vehicle : a physical *Life*-form; the physical (*beta*) body that is animated/controlled by the (*Alpha*) *Spirit* using a continuous *Spiritual Lifeline* (ZU); a physical (*beta*) organic receptacle and catalyst for the (*Alpha*) *Self* to operate "causes" and experience "effects" within the *Physical Universe*.

harmful-act : a counter-survival mode of behavior or action (esp. that causes harm to one of more *Spheres of Existence*)—or—an overtly aggressive (hostile and/or destructive) action against an individual or any other *Sphere of Existence*; in *Utilitarian Systemology*—a shortsighted (serves fewest/lowest *Spheres of Existence*) intentional overtly harmful action to resolve a perceived problem; a revision of the rule for standard *Utilitarianism* for Systemology to distinguish actions which provide the least benefit to the least number of *Spheres of Existence*, or else the greatest harm to the greatest number of *Spheres of Existence*; in *moral philosophy*—an action which can be experienced by few and/or which one would not be willing to experience for themselves (*theft, slander, rape, &tc*); an iniquity or iniquitous act.

hold-back : withheld communications (esp. actions) such as "*Hold-Outs*"; intentional (or automatic) withdrawal (as opposed to reach); Self-restraint (which may eventually be enforced or automated); not reaching, acting or expressing, when one should be; an ability that is now re-strained (on automatic) due to inability to with-hold it on Self-determinism alone.

hold-outs : in photography, the numerous snap-shots/pictures withheld from the final display or professional presentation of the event; withheld communications; in Utilitarian Systemology—energetic withdrawal and communication breaks with a "*terminal*" and its *Sphere of Existence* as a result of a "*Harmful-Act*"; unspoken or undis-covered (hidden, covert) actions that an indi-vidual withholds communications of, fearing punishment or endangerment of *Self-preserva-tion* (*First Sphere*); the act of hiding (or keeping hidden) the truth of a "*Harmful-Act*"; a refusal to communicate with a *Pilot*; also "*Hold-Back.*"

holistic : the examination of interconnected sys-tems as encompassing something greater than the *sum* of their "parts."

Human Condition : a standard default state of Human experience that is generally accepted to be the extent of its potential identity (*beingness*) —currently treated as *Homo Sapiens Sapiens,* but which is scheduled for replacement by *Homo Novus* (the "New Human").

imagination : ability to create *mental imagery* in one's Personal Universe at will and change or

89

alter it as desired; the ability to create, change and dissolve mental images on command or as an act of will; to create a mental image or have associated imagery displayed (or "conjured") in the mind that may or may not be treated as real (or memory recall) and may or may not accurately duplicate objective reality; to employ *creative abilities* of the Spirit that are independent of reality agreements with beta-existence.

imprint : to strongly impress, stamp, mark (or outline) onto a softer 'impressible' substance; to mark with pressure onto a surface; in *Systemology*, used to indicate permanent Reality impressions marked by frequencies, energies or interactions experienced during periods of emotional distress, pain, unconsciousness, loss, enforcement, or something antagonistic to physical (personal) survival, all of which are are stored with other reactive response-mechanisms at lower-levels of *Awareness* as opposed to the active memory database and proactive processing center of the Mind; an experiential "memory-set" that may later resurface—be triggered or stimulated artificially—as Reality, of which similar responses will be engaged automatically; holographic-like imagery "stamped" onto consciousness as composed of energetic *facets* tied to the "snap-shot" of an experience.

imprinting incident : the first or original event

instance communicated and *emotionally encoded* onto an individual's "*Spiritual Timeline*" (recorded memory from all lifetimes), which formed a permanent impression that is later used to mechanistically treat future contact on that channel; the first or original occurrence of some particular *facet* or mental image related to a certain type of *encoded response*, such as pain and discomfort, losses and victimization, and even the acts that we have taken against others along the *Spiritual Timeline* of our existence that caused them to also be *Imprinted*.

intention : directed application of Will; to intend (have "in Mind") or signify (give "significance" to) for or toward a particular purpose; in *Systemology* (from the *Standard Model*)—the spiritual activity at WILL (5.0) directed by an *Alpha Spirit* (7.0); the application of WILL as "Cause" from a higher order of Alpha Thought and consideration (6.0).

interior : inside of; on the inside; in *Systemology*, we mean specifically the POV of *Self* that is fixed to the *'internal' Human Condition,* including the *Reactive Control Center* (RCC) and Mind-System or *Master Control Center* (MCC); within *beta-existence*.

internal : a force coming from inside; information received from inside sources; in *Systemology*, the objective experience of *beta-existence* associated with the Physical Body or *genetic vehicle* and its POV regarding sensation and perception; from inside the body; in the body.

invalidate : decrease the level or degree or *agreement* as Reality.

mental image : a subjectively experienced "picture" created and imagined into being by the Alpha-Spirit (or at lower levels, one of its automated mechanisms) that includes all perceptible *facets* of totally immersive scene, which may be forms originated by an individual, or a "facsimile-copy" ("snap-shot") of something seen or encountered; a duplication of wave-forms in one's Personal Universe as a "picture" that mirror an "external" Universe experience, such as an *Imprint*.

perception : internalized processing of data received by the *senses*; to become *Aware of* via the senses.

pilot : a professional steersman responsible for healthy functional operation of a ship toward a specific destination; in *Systemology*, an intensive trained individual qualified to specially apply *Systemology Processing* to assist other *Seekers* on the *Pathway*.

point-of-view (POV) : a point to view from; an opinion or attitude as expressed from a specific identity-phase; a specific standpoint or vantage-point; a definitive manner of consideration specific to an individual phase or identity; a place or position affording a specific view or vantage; circumstances and programming of an individual that is conducive to a particular response, consideration or belief-set (paradigm); a position (consideration) or place (location) that provides a specific view or perspective (subjective) on experience (of the objective).

postulate : to put forward as truth; to suggest or assume an existence *to be*; to state or affirm the existence of particular conditions; to provide a basis of reasoning and belief; a basic theory accepted as fact; in *Systemology*, Alpha-Thought —the top-most decisions or considerations made by the Alpha-Spirit regarding the "*is-ness*" (what things "are") about energy-matter and space-time.

presence : a quality of some thing (*energy/matter*) being "present" in space-time; personal orientation of *Self* as an *Awareness* (*POV*) located in present space-time (environment) and communicating with extant energy-matter.

processing command line (PCL) : a directed input; a specific command using highly selective language for *Systemology Processing*; a predetermined directive statement (cause) intended to focus concentrated attention (effect).

processing, systematic : the inner-workings or "through-put" result of systems; in *Systemology*, a method of applied spiritual technology used toward personal Self-Actualization; methods of selective directed attention, communicated language and associative imagery that increases personal control of the human condition.

realization : the clear perception of an understanding; a consideration or understanding on what is "actual"; to make "real" or give "reality" to so as to grant a property of "beingness" or "being as it is"; the state or instance of coming to an *Awareness*; in *Systemology*, "gnosis" or true knowledge achieved during *systematic processing*; achievement of a new (or higher) cognition, true knowledge or perception of Self; a consideration of reality or assignment of meaning.

responsibility : the *ability* to *respond*; the extent of mobilizing *power* and *understanding* an individual maintains as *Awareness* to enact *change*; the proactive ability to *Self-direct* and make decisions independent of an outside authority.

Seeker : an individual on the *Pathway to Self-Honesty*; a practitioner of *Mardukite Systemology* or *Systemology Processing*, that is working toward *Spiritual Ascension*.

Self-actualization : bringing the full potential of the Human spirit into Reality; expressing full capabilities and creativeness of the *Alpha-Spirit*.

Self-determinism : the freedom to act, clear of external control or influence; the personal control of Will to direct intention.

Self-honesty : the basic or original *alpha* state of *being* and *knowing*; clear and present total *Awareness* of-and-as *Self*, in its most basic and true proactive expression of itself as *Spirit* or *I-AM*—free of artificial attachments, perceptive filters and other emotionally-reactive or mentally-conditioned programming imposed on the human condition by the systematized physical world; the ability to experience existence without judgment.

spiritual timeline : a continuous stream of moment-to-moment *Mental Images* (or a record of experiences) that defines the "past" of a spiritual being (or *Alpha-Spirit*) and which includes impressions (*imprints, &tc.*) from all life-incarnations and significant spiritual events the being has encountered; in Systemology, also "*backtrack.*"

Spheres of Existence : a series of *eight* concentric circles, rings or spheres (each larger than the former) that is overlaid onto the Standard Model of Beta-Existence to demonstrate the dynamic systems of existence extending out from the POV of Self (often as a "body") at the *First Sphere*; these are given in the basic eightfold systems as: *Self, Home/Family, Groups, Humanity, Life on Earth, Physical Universe, Spiritual Universe* and *Infinity-Divinity.*

Systemology : a modern tradition of applied religious philosophy and spiritual technology based on *Arcane Tablets* (in combination with "*general systemology*" and "*games theory*") developed in the New Age underground by Joshua Free in 2011 as an advanced futurist extension of the *Mardukite Research Org.*

terminal (node) : a point, end, or mass, on a line; a connection point for closing an electric circuit, such as a post on a battery terminating at each end of its own systematic function; a point of connectivity with other points; in systems, a contact point of interaction; a point of interaction with other points.

turbulence : a quality or state of distortion or disturbance that creates irregularity of a flow or pattern; the quality or state of aberration on a line (such as ragged edges) or the emotional "turbulent feelings" attached to a particular flow or terminal node; a violent, haphazard or disharmonious commotion (such as in the ebb of gusts and lulls of wind action).

validation : a reinforcement of agreements or considerations as being "real."

viewpoint : see *"point-of-view" (POV)*.

willingness : the state of conscious Self-determined ability and interest (directed attention) to *Be*, *Do* or *Have*; a Self-determined consideration to reach, face up to (*confront*) or manage some "mass" or energy; the extent to which an individual considers themselves able to participate, act or communicate along some line, to put attention or intention on the line, or to produce (create) an effect.

ZU : the ancient Sumerian cuneiform sign for the archaic verb—*"to know," "knowingness"* or *"awareness"*; in *Mardukite Zuism and Systemology*, the active energy/matter of the "Spiritual Universe" (AN) experienced as a *Lifeforce* or *consciousness* that imbues living forms extant in the "Physical Universe" (KI); *"Spiritual Life Energy"*; energy demonstrated by the WILL of an actualized *Alpha-Spirit* in the "Spiritual Universe" (AN), which impinges its *Awareness* into the Physical Universe (KI), animating/controlling *Life* for its experience of *beta-existence* along an individual Alpha-Spirit's personal *Identity-continuum*, called a *ZU-line*.

Zu-Line : a theoretical construct in *Mardukite Zuism and Systemology* demonstrating *Spiritual*

Life Energy (*ZU*) as a personal individual "continuum" of Awareness interacting with all Spheres of Existence on the Standard Model of Systemology; a spectrum of potential variations and interactions of a monistic continuum or singular *Spiritual Life Energy* demonstrated on the Standard Model; an energetic channel of potential POV and "locations" of Beingness, demonstrated in early Systemology materials as an individual Alpha-Spirit's personal *Identity- continuum*, potentially connecting *Awareness* of *Self* with "*Infinity*" simultaneous with all points considered in existence; a symbolic demonstration of the "*Life-line*" on which *Awareness (ZU)* extends from the direction of the "Spiritual Universe" (AN) in its true original *alpha state* through an entire possible range of activity resulting in its *beta state* and control of a *genetic-entity* occupying the *Physical Universe (KI).*

Zu-Vision : the true and basic (*Alpha*) Point-of-View (perspective, POV) maintained by *Self* as *Alpha-Spirit* outside boundaries or considerations of the *Human Condition* and *exterior* to beta-existence reality agreements with the Physical Universe; a POV of Self *as* "a unit of Spiritual Awareness" that exists independent of a "body" and entrapment in a *Human Condition*; "spirit vision" in its truest sense.

explore the
Fundamentals of Systemology

All *six*
Basic Course
lesson booklets
in one
hardcover
edition!

start your journey on the
The Pathway to Ascension

All *sixteen*
Professional Course
lesson booklets
in two
hardcover
volumes!

THE SYSTEMOL

Seekers and students of the *Basic Course* and *Professional Course* will also be interested in the *Systemology Core Research Series.* These eight volumes are a complete chronological record of the Mardukite New Thought developments from the Systemology Society, published in 2019 through 2023.

The *Systemology Core* begins with the first professional publication released when the *Mardukite Systemology Society* emerged from the underground in 2019, with: *"The Tablets of Destiny Revelation."*

OGY PATHWAY

The Tablets of Destiny Revelation:
*How Long-Lost Anunnaki Wisdom
Can Change the Fate of Humanity*

Crystal Clear: *Handbook for Seekers*

Metahuman Destinations (*2 volumes*)

Imaginomicon:
Approaching Gateways to Higher Universes

Way of the Wizard: *Utilitarian Systemology*

Systemology-180: *Fast-Track to Ascension*

Systemology Backtrack:
Reclaiming Spiritual Power & Past-Life Memory

PUBLISHED BY THE **JOSHUA FREE** IMPRINT REPRESENTING

The Mardukite Academy of Systemology

THE JOSHUA FREE IMPRINT
JFI PUBLICATIONS

MARDUKITE
ZUISM

mardukite.com

www.ingramcontent.com/pod-product-compliance
Lightning Source LLC
Chambersburg PA
CBHW071208120626
46546CB00006B/2478